FEROCIOUS FIGHTING ANIMALS

WILD BOARS

Julia J. Quinlan

PowerKiDS
press™

New York

Published in 2013 by The Rosen Publishing Group, Inc.
29 East 21st Street, New York, NY 10010

First Edition

Editor: Amelie von Zumbusch
Book Design: Andrew Povolny

Photo Credits: Cover Sven Zacek/Oxford Scientific/Getty Images; pp. 4, 21 iStockphoto/Thinkstock; p. 5 Cordier Sylvain/hemis.fr/Getty Images; pp. 6–7 Sven–Erik Arndt/Picture Press/Getty Images; pp. 8, 10–11, 12–13, 16–17 FotoVeto/Shutterstock.com; p. 9 © Eric Isseleé - Fotolia.com; p. 14 Jaroslav Pesat/Shutterstock.com; p. 15 Radka Palenikova/Shutterstock.com; p. 18 Jupiterimages/Photos.com/Thinkstock; p. 19 Eduard Kyslynskyy/Shutterstock.com; p. 20 Arpi/Shutterstock.com; p. 22 Joe McDonald/Visuals Unlimited/Getty Images.

Publisher Cataloging Data

Quinlan, Julia J.
      Wild boars / Julia J. Quinlan.
p.   cm. — (Ferocious fighting animals) — 1st ed.
Includes index.
Summary: This book tells about wild boars, big scary pigs found in many locations and habitats, including physical characteristics, what they eat, and how they raise their young.
Contents: Tough pigs — Wild boars everywhere – Tusks and more — Boars living together — Ferocious wild boars — Piglets and growing up — Not picky eaters — Predators — Boars and people — Seemingly safe.
      ISBN 978-1-4488-9676-9 (library binding) — ISBN 978-1-4488-9810-7 (pbk.)
ISBN 978-1-4488-9811-4 (6-pack)
      1. Wild boar—Juvenile literature   [1. Wild boar]   I. Title
            2013
      599.63/32—dc23

Manufactured in the United States of America

CPSIA Compliance Information: Batch #W13PK5: For Further Information contact Rosen Publishing, New York, New York at 1-800-237-9932

CONTENTS

TOUGH PIGS

Wild boars go by many different names. They are known as razorbacks, wild pigs, and wild swine. People call them different things depending on where they live. Wild boars are related to the pigs found on farms. They are not pink or cute, though. Wild boars are big, scary pigs. Wild boars can be found in many different places. Wherever they are, people have to be careful not to get in their way!

Wild boars tend to have longer snouts than pigs on farms do.

Wild boars are brave. They do not run away when they are threatened. They stay and fight. They use their size and sharp **tusks** to defend themselves.

As other pigs do, wild boars wallow, or roll, in mud to keep cool and keep away insects.

5

WILD BOARS EVERYWHERE

Wild boars are one of the most widely **distributed** animals. That means they live in more places than most animals. Wild boars were originally found in Europe, Asia, and North Africa. Over time, people brought them to other places. Wild boars now live in South America, North America, South Africa, and many other places.

Wild boars live in many **habitats**, such as forests, woodlands, shrubland, grasslands, and farmland. Wild boars like to live in places that are not too hot and not too cold. They also like to live in places that get a good amount of rain.

Most of the wild boars that live in Europe live in forests, as this mother boar and her piglets do.

TUSKS AND MORE

Wild boars are very large. They tend to weigh between 110 and 770 pounds (50–349 kg)! They can be 20 to 36 inches (51–91 cm) tall. Male wild boars are usually larger than females. Wild boars have coarse, wiry hair that can be dark gray to brown.

The thicker hairs in a wild boar's coat are known as bristles.

Boars have snouts and ears like farm pigs do. They also have tails. Their tails vary in length.

Wild boars have tusks that grow larger as they age. Most wild boars have four tusks that grow from their jaws. The tusks are very sharp. Males have much larger teeth than females do.

Wild boars have hooves with two toes. These are also known as cloven hooves.

BOARS LIVING TOGETHER

A group of wild boars is called a **sounder**. Sounders usually have about 6 to 20 boars but can have as many as 100. Sounders are made up of female wild boars and their young. Sounders travel together in their **home range**.

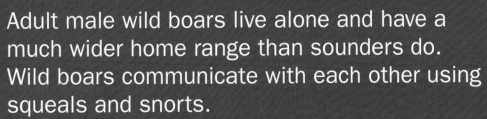

Adult male wild boars live alone and have a much wider home range than sounders do. Wild boars communicate with each other using squeals and snorts.

Wild boars have very strong senses of smell and taste. Scientists think wild boars do not have very good eyesight. Their eyes are on the sides of their faces, so they cannot see forward very well.

Wild boars tend to be most active in the early morning and late afternoon. In places where there are many people, they may be most active at night.

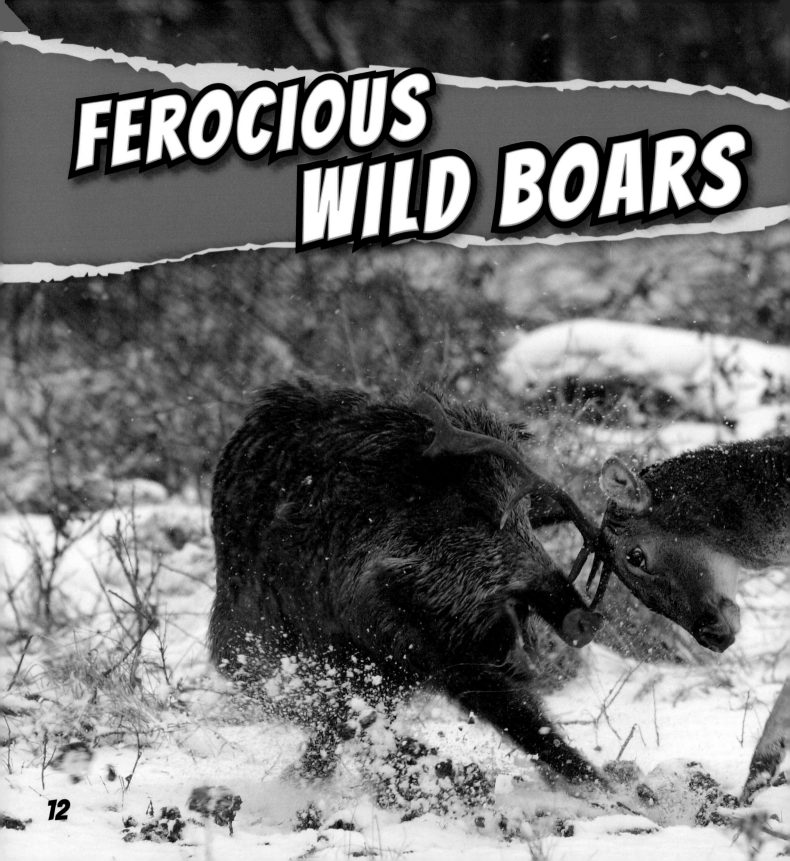

FEROCIOUS WILD BOARS

Wild boars are tough fighters. They fearlessly charge at animals with which they are fighting. Wild boars are known for goring their opponents, or stabbing them with their sharp tusks. They have even been known to kill people who were hunting them!

PIGLETS AND GROWING UP

During **mating** season, male wild boars fight each other over female wild boars. These fights can get very violent. Male boars that win more fights get to mate with more females. Wild boars mate at different times depending on where they live.

These male wild boars are fighting over which one will get to mate with a female.

Wild boar piglets have stripes. This helps them blend in with the plants around them, which makes them harder for predators to spot.

Female wild boars give birth to litters of 1 to 12 piglets. Wild boars give birth in special nests made of grass. Piglets stay with their mothers for up to a year. They drink milk from their mothers for the first three to four months. Mother wild boars are very protective of their young.

NOT PICKY EATERS

Wild boars eat almost anything. They eat insects, reptiles, **fungi**, eggs, vegetables, and much more! Wild boars are particularly fond of fruit. They will eat the bodies of dead animals as well as **dung**. They use their strong sense of smell to track down food. They sometimes use their sharp hooves to dig for food. Wild boars will gather together to eat. Even adult males that live on their own will sometimes eat with other boars.

Wild boars' ability to eat anything has helped them live in so many places. They can always find something that they like to eat.

Wild boars are good at digging up roots and other underground foods. As they do with most of their food, the boars find underground foods by smell.

PREDATORS

Wild boars have different predators depending on where they live. Crocodiles, bears, and large cats have been known to kill adult wild boars. Piglets are at the greatest risk of being killed by predators. Mother wild boars fight fiercely to protect their piglets. However, wolves, large birds, and snakes sometimes kill piglets.

In places where both wild boars and tigers live, wild boars are an important source of food for tigers.

Wild boars usually leave people alone. When they do attack people, they tend to attack people who are hunting them.

Wild boars are very **aggressive** when threatened. Females are most aggressive when their piglets are around. Males are most aggressive during the mating season. They try to stab enemies with their sharp tusks. They sharpen their tusks by rubbing the upper tusks against the lower tusks.

BOARS AND PEOPLE

Humans are the main predators of wild boars. People hunt wild boars for food and sport. Wild boar meat is popular in some countries. In these countries, there are farms where wild boars are raised for food. Wild boar meat can be quite expensive.

Wild boars can be very destructive to crops. They root up bulbs and seeds. They also eat growing crops.

Hunting wild boars is a popular sport in many places.

Wild boars died out in England but were brought back and now live there again. Wild boars were accidentally introduced to Canada and the United States. There, they are an **invasive species**. Invasive species are bad for the animals and plants that naturally live in a place. Wild boars in North America are often hunted to control their **populations**.

SEEMINGLY SAFE

Wild boars are not **endangered**. Overall, their population numbers are high. However, wild boar populations are shrinking in some areas. Wild boars could become threatened in those places.

Wild boars can live in many habitats and will eat just about anything. These ferocious pigs should not be messed with! Because they are so tough, people sometimes forget that some populations of wild boars need to be protected. Luckily, there are several national parks and nature reserves where they can live in their natural habitats.

National parks are a great place to see wild boars in their natural habitats. This wild boar is in Bandhavgarh National Park, in Madhya Pradesh, India.

GLOSSARY

aggressive (uh-GREH-siv) Ready to fight.

distributed (dih-strih-BYOOT-ed) Spread out.

dung (DUNG) Animal waste.

endangered (in-DAYN-jerd) In danger of no longer existing.

fungi (FUN-jy) Plantlike living things that do not have leaves, flowers, or green color and that do not make their own food.

habitats (HA-buh-tats) The kinds of land where animals or plants naturally live.

home range (HOHM RAYNJ) The area in which an animal usually stays.

invasive species (in-VAY-siv SPEE-sheez) Plants or animals that are brought to a place and drive out the plants and animals that naturally live there.

mating (MAY-ting) Coming together to make babies.

populations (pop-yoo-LAY-shunz) Groups of animals or people living in the same place.

sounder (SOWN-der) A group of wild boars, warthogs, or other animals in the pig family.

tusks (TUSKS) Long, large pointed teeth that come out of the mouths of some animals.

INDEX

WEBSITES

Due to the changing nature of Internet links, PowerKids Press has developed an online list of websites related to the subject of this book. This site is updated regularly. Please use this link to access the list: www.powerkidslinks.com/ffa/boar/